PLATFORM PAPERS

QUARTERLY ESSAYS ON THE PERFORMING ARTS FROM CURRENCY HOUSE

No. 63
March 2021

Platform Papers Partners

We acknowledge with gratitude our Partners in continuing support of Platform Papers and its mission to widen understanding of performing arts practice and encourage change when it is needed:

Neil Armfield, AO
Anita Luca Belgiorno-Nettis Foundation
Jane Bridge
Katharine Brisbane, AM
Elizabeth Butcher, AM
Penny Chapman
Dr Peter Cooke, AM
Sally Crawford
Wesley Enoch
Ferrier Hodgson
Larry Galbraith
Wayne Harrison, AM
Campbell Hudson
Lindy Hume
Professors Bruce King and Denise Bradley, AC
Justice François Kunc
Dr Richard Letts, AM
Peter Lowry, OAM and Carolyn Lowry, OAM
David Marr
Helen O'Neil
Lesley Power
Professor William Purcell
Queensland Performing Arts Centre Trust
Geoffrey Rush, AC
Dr Merilyn Sleigh
Maisy Stapleton
Augusta Supple
Christopher Tooher
Caroline Verge
Queensland Performing Arts Trust
Rachel Ward, AM and Bryan Brown, AM
Kim Williams, AM
Professor Di Yerbury, AM

Platform Paper No. 63 has been produced with the generous support of the University of Sydney

To them and to all subscribers and Friends of Currency House we extend our grateful thanks.

Platform Papers Readers' Forum

Like many, Currency House suspended its operations during the crisis caused by the Covid-19 pandemic, including the publication of Platform Papers, but we have not been idle. We have used the time, while the office has been closed, to refresh our thinking, reflect on the work of the last two decades and restructure. We resume the series in 2021 with the launch of Platform Paper no. 63: *On the Lessons of History*, by our patron and founder, Katharine Brisbane; and reopen with a new executive. Katharine's daughter, Harriet Parsons, takes up the role of Director, and Julian Meyrick, the general editorship of Platform Papers.

We are also pleased to announce that we are reissuing the entire backlist of Platform Papers in a new electronic edition, available through most university libraries. The edition will make it easier for teachers to design courses around the collection with improved functions for students and researchers. Hard copies of the Papers will continue to be available through the Currency Press website www.currency.com.au.

The pandemic continues at the time of publication, but as the emergency measures begin to be lifted, the national focus is turning towards recovery and adaptation to a changed future. Rather than picking up where we left off, we have decided to make 2021 a year of review, with a mid-year creative convention with all our authors, friends and supporters at the University of Sydney. Having published 62 innovative plans for improving conditions in the arts over the past sixteen years, in 2021 we are introducing a program of support for bringing these plans to fruition.

Readers' responses to our essays would normally be posted on our website, but this will be temporarily replaced by a minimal homepage, and the new design will be launched at the convention. However the Editor will still be welcoming your responses which may be incorporated into some of the sessions. Contributions of 250 to 2,000 words, headed 'Reader response' in the subject field, may be e-mailed to info@currencyhouse.org.au.

We will be reviewing all of Currency House's programs in 2021, including the format and frequency of Platform Papers. This year we will be publishing one more issue summarising the results of the convention, before we start a new series in 2022.

ON THE LESSONS OF HISTORY

KATHARINE BRISBANE

ABOUT THE AUTHOR

Katharine Brisbane is a writer and publisher who co-founded Currency Press, Australia's performing arts publisher, with her late husband, Dr Philip Parsons, in 1971. She was a theatre critic for 21 years, including a period as national critic of the *Australian* (1967–1974), a time of radical change that saw the rise of contemporary drama, film and music in Australia. She has published widely on the history and nature of Australian theatre. She remained publisher of Currency Press until her retirement in 2001 and at that time established Currency House, Inc., a not-for-profit association with the brief to assert the value of the performing arts in public life and raise the level of debate.

She was a founder in 1972 of the Australian National Playwrights' Conference and was Chair from 1985–1990. In 1991 to celebrate Currency Press's first twenty years she edited *Entertaining Australia*, a social history of the performing arts. In 1993 Katharine and Philip were both awarded the AM for their work as publishers of Australian drama. Dr Parsons died the same month and Katharine completed the production of his encyclopaedia, *Companion to Theatre in Australia*, published in 1995. She holds honorary doctorates from the University of NSW and the University of WA, and many awards for her writing and publishing, including the Dorothy Crawford Award by the Australian Writers' Guild for outstanding service to the Australian playwright, and lifetime achievement awards from Melbourne's Green Room, the Sydney Critics Circle, and in 2009 a Special Award from the NSW Premier in the Literary Awards list for services to Australian literature and theatre.

From 1994 she was editor for the South Pacific for the *World Encyclopaedia of Contemporary Theatre* (Routledge), for which she also wrote the Australian entry. *Volume 5: Asia and the Pacific* was published in 1998. She has written widely in books and journals and a collection of her writings, *Not Wrong, Just Different: Observations on the rise of the contemporary theatre*, was published in 2005.

Katharine Brisbane has two children: Nicholas, a film-maker, and Harriet, an artist and independent researcher; and two granddaughters.

Foreword

This is to be my last Platform Paper. Age and uncertain health brought about my decision in December 2019 to retire from the daily administration of Currency House. For some time we had been working on arrangements to secure the Papers' future under the aegis of a public institution, but from 2015 onwards, the political climate of arts funding and sponsorship had been steadily retreating. When the Covid-19 pandemic crept upon us in March 2020, we had already cancelled the Arts and Creativity breakfasts and we now suspended all our operations including the Papers. My daughter, Harriet Parsons, took advantage of the months of inactivity to restructure Currency House and find a permanent solution to our problems.

So in 2021 we are starting again. Julian Meyrick, a long-time friend and associate of Currency House, and now Professor of Creative Studies at Griffith University, has accepted the role of general editor of Platform Papers and Harriet has taken on the job of Director.

It only remains for me to thank full-heartedly all those who helped in wrangling together the myriad parts of this paper. Harriet was an essential part of achieving its finished form, in helping me to wrestle the detail of the material and clarify the moving timeline;

and Julian Meyrick for using his understanding of our cultural history to support my argument. My thanks, equally, go to the other members of the Currency House Board and editorial committee for their support as we devised a way forward for Platform Papers at this time of cultural crisis. It's been a pleasure and a challenge to bring together the strength of all these creative voices and I hope they will be heard far and wide as we take this unique opportunity to together imagine Australia as a wiser and more creative country.

Introduction

It was the best of times. It was the worst of times. The millennium had just turned. Expectations of disaster had run high: about whether the mysterious new digital technology, on which we had so quickly come to depend, would bring the world to an end at midnight on 31 December? Its instrument was to be the algorithm in charge of the world's clocks, which had defined the date during the old century by two digits (99) and had to be revised to four (2000). Digital conversion, as we all came to understand, was not flexible, like the human brain. The change would transform the whole of world commerce, even as the rise of the digital age laid out a new world before us. Were we to call this first decade of the twenty-first century the noughties?

This paper ruminates on the concerns that have occupied the arts sector in Australia during this century so far: the decisions we have made, the disasters we have survived and the opportunities that are now open to make us a kinder, more congenial society. The reader will have deduced, if they are not old enough to remember, that the end of the world did not occur at midnight on 31 December 1999. How many of our other expectations have changed since then?

Who could have imagined twenty years ago that a virus, uncovered in a wet market in China, would spread right round the world in 2020, and reach epic proportions in the space of three or four months? The pandemic continues at the time of writing but the forced hiatus has given us time at Currency House to refresh our thinking, reflect on the work of the past two decades and restructure.

To this end I have gathered up the 62 Platform Papers and begun an overview of their contribution to the events that have impacted upon the arts since the Millennium. Not every paper has made it into the finished text but each has brought fresh insight into the reasons why the nation's creative instinct has, in our view, been systematically suppressed. And the full list is printed with the Endnotes.

In great part the picture in the arts has been of a young country, of colonial origins, that for most of its history has refused to recognise the creative management of the land practised by our First Nations people and blindly deferred to the customary practices of its great and powerful friends. And who today amid extraordinary global change is timidly attempting to transform our old structure as a middle-sized nation trading primary goods into an intellectual, multicultural global thinker.

The exploration has left me with one question in particular. Why, at the start, when the Government set up a system in support of the creative arts in 1968, was the Australia Council's funding directed at the product rather than the creator? In the first year of the life of the Australia Council, those of us who were there, with a head full of ideas but too little experience, grasped at a huge opportunity to shape the future of the arts. Jean Battersby, as founding director of the Council, proposed that for funding and management purposes we should divide up the arts sector by genre or 'artform', a shoddy word that has regulated Council planning ever since. Art is a quality that can be applied to a myriad of forms but has no form of its own. It is an expression of certain values. This decision made the 'form' the focus of the Boards that were duly set up, rather than artists and their needs. As artists experimented, the 'artforms' proliferated; and projects were regularly rejected because they 'fell outside the guidelines'. As a result, over time, the output has been allowed to overshadow the benefit to society of artists themselves.

As Dorothy Hewett once said to me, art is the detritus of the creative process. Valuing the product over the creator places the Australia Council in the same category as Centrelink. It asks our artists to 'work for hours': that is, to allocate their time in a way that will enable a profitable outcome. Some creative people have devised such a way to make a living. Some have even prospered. But how many of these fortunate creators count the value of their practice in terms of hourly cost? My guess is that they would say they work at their chosen practice because they cannot do otherwise. It is their vocation.

When we arrived at the turn of the century, the last decade had been a nervous one. Paul Keating's Labor

Government had given us a rush of radical reforms: the Native Title Act, compulsory superannuation, enterprise bargaining, privatisation of QANTAS and the Commonwealth Bank, the creation of APEC and a Republic Advisory Committee. There had been much to digest. So in 1996, for those who voted him in, John Howard's promise of 'relaxed and comfortable' government came as a welcome relief. The Coalition won a massive 45-seat majority and Australia settled down to the prospect of a reliable, if rather boring, decade.

However, within weeks we were shaken from this dream by what came to be known as the Port Arthur Massacre. Martin Bryant's rampage on 28 April 1996, left 35 dead, many more wounded and holds the record for the worst mass murder in modern Australian history. Howard's swift action on gun control caught voters by surprise; but the moral authority he won by his handling of that event was squandered in 2001, on the eve of his third term as prime minister, by the stand he took against the Norwegian vessel MV *Tampa.* Its Captain, Arne Rinnan, had rescued 433 mainly Afghan refugees from a fishing vessel in international waters off our north-west coast. When he attempted to land them on Christmas Island SAS troops were ordered to board the ship.

Howard's hard line on the refugees was vindicated in the eyes of the popular press when, a month later, on 11 September 2001, two hijacked American Airlines planes, and their helpless passengers, smashed into Manhattan's World Trade Center, killing 3,000 men and women as they descended on New York's financial heart at the beginning of a working day. We knew that our safe, parochial, middle power, so far from the fears of the world's trouble spots, would never be the same.

I had dined at the Windows on the World restaurant in the North Tower of the World Trade Centre only months before the attack. My companion and I stood looking down at the ant-like figures scurrying along the street below, like Harry Lime on the Ferris wheel in *The Third Man*.[1] 'No wonder the Americans think they are masters of the world,' I said. But the world no longer thinks so today.

Where was I when I heard the news of this world-changing massacre? I had sold our family home and awoke that morning in my friend Jean Cooney's apartment to the sound of the radio urging us to turn on the television. We watched, hypnotised, as first one and then the other twin tower crumbled almost silently. It happened so slowly we could see the victims as they fell from the windows. That day I closed the door on 87 Jersey Road, Woollahra, which had been my home for 35 years, and the place where Philip and I had established Currency Press, with Jean as my colleague and assistant. Currency and I were now awaiting the completion of the Press's new offices in Cleveland Street, Redfern, to which we were adding a rooftop apartment for me. Closing one more door meant opening another.

In October, the Government claimed that refugees from another vessel were now threatening to throw their children overboard. The claim was proved false; but in November, another election secured another substantial majority for the Coalition. Howard summarily introduced and passed his Border Protection Bill and the *Tampa's* Afghan refugees were deported to Nauru. Over Christmas, in a mixture of excitement and weariness, the Currency staff and I moved into our new home.

In October 2002 Australians experienced the horrors of terrorism firsthand. The Bali bombing of a popular tourist site killed 88 Australians, 38 Indonesians and 28 Britons; and their personal stories were published beside those of asylum seekers in the media. The rising tide of refugees escalated public concern for their safety as they risked their lives on the way to Australia. At the same time, it also heightened Islamophobia. Our refugee policy, once seen as contributing to economic growth, was transforming our reputation by leaps and shocks, from a welcoming nation, made up of generations of immigrants, into one that builds detention centres and imposes regulations to ensure that 'we decide who comes to our country and the manner in which they come'.[2]

As opinion polarised we began to lose our trust in the society we thought we understood. *What kind of Australia are we becoming?* we wondered.

John Howard continued in office until 2007 when Labor under Kevin Rudd won a crushing victory ('Kevin '07') in which Howard himself lost his seat of Bennelong to Walkley award-winning journalist Maxine McKew. Rudd's elevation excited public expectations: here was a new breed of parliamentarian, one fluent in Chinese, who would lead reform and strengthen our ties with Asia and the Pacific. Peter Garrett, lawyer and rock star, became a high profile Minister in a number of portfolios. His role as Arts Minister raised particular hopes; a familiar face and someone who knew what living as a performer was like, but the pace of reform came too fast. 'Mistakes were made', as they say; Rudd alienated his allies and it all fell apart in a coup.

Labor did not reverse the policy on refugees.

Two distinct forces have shaped the changes since 2000. The first is the digital world, which encouraged autonomy and social fragmentation; the second, the voice of growing Aboriginal authority. At the start, the internet, which allowed anyone to publish an opinion online, was seen as a triumph of democracy; but mass online publishing diminished the profits of the print publishers by delivering their content free, and undermined their authority by discarding the supervision of editors.

It has also given rise to 'trolling', the fatal flaw in social media. Traditional publishers have policies about what they will and will not publish; the social media have armies of 'moderators' instead, who take offensive information down, but only after it has been published and the damage is already done. Editors protect civil society. Their loss has been especially bad for newspapers. Today, newspapers who once delivered authoritative journalism compete with the digital media to deliver intimate, heart-breaking stories via multiple portals in vibrant colour and with breathless speed.

Since September 11, the media's capacity to bring death and disaster, triumph and glory, to our living rooms, has never been so great.

But as the authority of the press has fragmented, one voice has grown in strength and unity: that of our Indigenous leaders, including in the performing arts. Steady progress was made towards reconciliation in the 1980s and 1990s, including the establishment of a Council for Aboriginal Reconciliation, the Mabo decision, which rejected the historical fiction of *terra nullius*; and on 28 May 2000, over five hours, 250,000 people walked across the Sydney Harbour Bridge in the cause of reconciliation. There were similar events in Brisbane and Melbourne.

But in 2007 this goodwill was dealt a blow when allegations of widespread sexual abuse of Aboriginal children were made by the Victorian State Crown Prosecutor, Nanette Rogers, SC. This led Howard to order the Northern Territory National Emergency Response. Little was achieved. The unexpected deployment of Army troops against Australian citizens only revived traumatic memories for the Stolen Generations of the forcible removal of children from their parents. A decade later, it was the energetic management of those Aboriginal elders who signed the Uluru Statement from the Heart that finally began to break down the walls of mutual fear and anger that had for so long been a major hindrance to healthy debate.

The Uluru Statement is a simple, moving document, composed for the 2017 First Nations National

Constitutional Convention on the lands of the Anangu people and accepted by consensus of all 250 delegates. It has become a familiar point of reference, a guide to quiet conversation between multicultural Australia and its first nations.

Publications by Indigenous authors, like Bruce Pascoe's *Dark Emu* (2014), broke through the racial divide of unthinking oppression in other ways, by bringing their research into the body of knowledge about cultural and agricultural science, astronomy, fire, drought and flood management, family and social harmony, and moral regulation. Given the evidence of historical injustice, the squabbling in Parliament and lack of even basic courtesy shown by our then Prime Minister Malcolm Turnbull's swift rejection of the Statement from the Heart, it is astonishing that our indigenous elders have still found a means to prevail with their soft voices. The Uluru Statement will not go away.

For Australia this has been a period of cultural change from which we have emerged a different nation. So far we have learnt much about how power works but nothing about how to wield it on the global stage. We only know that the giant act of vandalism called September 11 surpassed anything we had known before. In the years since 2001, we have allowed ourselves to become swept up in our fears and occupied with distractions—new devices of incomprehensible ingenuity that invite entry into dazzling new worlds to escape the wreck we have made of this one. It has taken until 2020 for a new kind of change—drought, floods, earthquakes, famine and now global plague—for our stubborn hearts to make the turn towards a more rational way of life and public and community trust.

1. The Genesis of the Papers

In the 1970s, arts support expanded under the aegis of the Australia Council, and by the 1980s artists and arts organisations were largely dependent on regular government grants, but when funding began to contract in the 1990s, this dependence made practitioners fearful of speaking out. By the turn of the twenty-first century global upheaval and political polarisation were also increasing the mood of despondency among arts workers. Something was needed to restore, from the fragments of our culture, the arts' mirror on the world. We needed a national conversation about the breadth of artistic endeavour and why we define it as part of the common good. So in 2001 my colleagues and I began a monthly discussion club in Sydney and called it Currency House. We became a not-for-profit affiliate of Currency Press, which also gave us a home.

But the silence that had possessed so many working artists meant that persuading people to talk about their problems was not easy. Self-esteem was low, confessing weakness inadmissible: however desperate things got, it was a professional necessity for artists to appear always 'in demand', a hollow defence of the itinerant worker to prevent temporary unemployment becoming permanent.

We solved the problem by introducing the Chatham House rule to our monthly debates. The public issues thus raised in private became the inspiration, in 2004, for a quarterly essay dedicated to the working life of those in the creative sector (as it has come to be called) and the support systems on which they depend. We settled on four issues a year supported by a committee under the general editorship of the plan's initiator, Dr John Golder from the School of Theatre Studies at the University of NSW.

Reading the earliest papers again in 2020, in which we set out to document the causes of the malaise, I am astounded by the authors' percipience. They exude a pent-up energy and courage in their targeting of social causes and proposals for betterment. But even more surprising is the accuracy of the forecasts. Disappointingly, for those who shared those early days with me, few of their innovations (or good intentions) have yet been vested in public policy. To those in the know, this is no surprise.

In the last twelve months we have experienced fire and flood, the greatest modern Australia has seen, followed by the Covid-19 pandemic, which within four months silently swept around the world, dividing families, causing myriad deaths, closing business and entertainment, and locking down state borders and communities. Governments are now working overtime to find ways to save the economy.

The continuing months of isolation have brought a change in priorities and even a change of heart about the purpose of the public money that furnishes federal and state incomes, and the importance of social policy over productive employment, in times of depression or disaster. The succession of shocks that landed on an unprepared nation, has forced the disturbing realisation on Australians that we are no longer protected by distance from our global responsibilities, nor excluded from its dangers. With remarkable stoicism the Coalition's leaders have released billions of dollars, not just to those seeking a job, but for those seeking a life.

But now that it looks as though another year may pass before we see the back of this pandemic, panicky voices are beginning to rise, fearful of the changes this global pause for thought will bring about. As in the early days of the Platform Papers, now is the time for a proper national conversation: to listen, to speak out, and to be heard.

2. Coordinating the Voices

The Platform Papers series quickly became a record of the mood of the times. The aim was not to write a history series but to add to our understanding of the present and ways to bring about a better future. The brief to authors became a four-point structure comprising an account of

1. the state of the subject under scrutiny;
2. its history and social causes;
3. new directions that might be taken; and finally,
4. a challenge to the reader with a new idea or provocation to move forward.

This has proved a sound framework on which to hang 60-plus issues over 16 years. The authors' chosen themes have ranged from industry work practices to environmental sustainability, public policy, export, finance, censorship, copyright, welfare and all genres of the performing arts including film, television and an increasing variety of digital media.

The need for change has been expressed palpably in each paper. Each has met a challenge, sometimes receiving criticism, at other times gratitude for enabling an important argument to be heard. The question of what it means to be an Australian, and where this leads us, haunts them all.

What follows will give a brief insight into the principal issues that have preoccupied our authors. We asked them to raise new, provocative questions about the purpose of the arts and the conditions under which artists work. The first authors we approached responded with a cautious promise to think it over, but once they began, the writing came like a long exhale of breath, leaving them exhausted and exhilarated, although still fearful of standing up to defend their precarious way of life.

The Rise of the Digital Realm

At the outset the rise and rise of the digital realm was hailed as the discovery of a new democratic playing field for the creative mind. The technological change came with frightening speed and power. 2004 to 2006 saw the launch of the social media platforms Facebook, YouTube and Twitter. Digital expansion allowed anyone to publish an opinion, instantly world-wide, in exchange for no more than their personal data—name, city, date of birth, and what they 'like'. The flood of 'free' information undermined the profits of the commercial media and put news organisations in particular under pressure. It also detached publishing in the public domain from the 'gatekeepers' of copyright protection, journalistic integrity and censorship.

By 2010 we had come to realise the ruthlessness of the game we were in, the all-consuming nature of the new technology, and it changed the face of arts publishing forever. Shilo McClean was exhilarated by the vision of the new democratic creative freedom the digital realm offered—the chance for all of us to be creative—but warned of the way the corporate world was engaging with innovation in PP No.24, *The Digital Playing Fields: New rulz for film art and performance*. New stores of data stretched beyond imagination, but the pressing challenge now was how to ensure that the daily news was reliable:

> *It is an established pattern that innovation is followed by commercial exploitation, which eventually trends to a situation of monopoly or duopoly in the control of production. The pattern is so common one might even think it inevitable. Indeed, it could be argued that the ensuing stagnation that arises once a field is dominated by powerbrokers is in fact a condition that is a prerequisite for further innovation.* PP24, pp.5–6

By 2020 uncertainty had become a way of life. Having learned to live with flexible employment and flexible income, we now have to negotiate 'fake news'. In 2004 the author of PP No.1, Martin Harrison, was already sounding the alarm. He was the founding producer of the ABC's *Radio Arts* (now defunct) and presenter of *Books and Writing*. In *'Our ABC' a Dying Culture? One way forward in arts programming*, he warned:

> *The ABC is not fulfilling its Charter obligations in relation to the arts. There is a long history of budget cuts, poor management appointments, poor policy decisions, Federal Government interference and a lack-lustre Board, which lie, in large measure, behind the declining significance of the ABC.* PP1, p.1

The Australian Broadcasting Corporation, founded in the 1930s as the Australian Broadcasting Commission, was modelled on the BBC with its Charter of objectives.[3] As the independent dispenser of free public information, the ABC's charter was intended to protect it from external pressures, but an ever-shrinking budget, coupled with performance measures based on commercial standards, meant that it was struggling to serve the public good. Inexplicably, profit had somehow taken over from ethics as the measure of good governance. The metaphor, so deplored by economists, that governments, like households, must live within their means, had reframed the arts as entertainment—an indulgence that should be foregone in difficult times—rather than an indispensable asset of a thinking society.

Harrison's modest suggestions for enlarging the arts coverage were politely received and ignored and ABCTV programming began to include an increasingly large proportion of safe British 'bonnet' dramas. Today, in the commercial sector, the channels survive, but with only a shadow of their former ratings.

In 2009 Ian David, veteran screenwriter and director of many award-winning series, gave an insider's view of the television industry in his PP No.21, *Television: What will rate in the new tomorrow?* On-line streaming had forced the free-to-air services to seek out new ways of attracting audiences and he deplored the flood of 'reality TV' shows and general decline in the quality of content—but he concluded that, despite the assault on its ratings, television was here to stay.

Kim Dalton, a former Head of ABC Television, again tackled the issue of the ABC's integrity in 2017, reporting bitterly that there had been no favourable advance since he left in 2013. In PP No.51, *Missing in Action: The ABC and Australia's screen culture*, he too deplored the reduction in local production and argued that the ABC Charter was outdated, with no provision for transparency or accountability.

> *The only guidance in regard to Australia's cultural output and its creative community is the requirement that it should 'encourage and promote the musical, dramatic and other performing arts in Australia'. Arguably a very narrow, somewhat old-fashioned, and potentially elitist, instruction that ignores whole areas of contemporary creative practice including screen production. Beyond the Charter, though, there is no indication from government of just what the ABC is meant to do, how it is meant to do it and to what end.* PP51, p.35

In 2020, however, the Covid-19 pandemic has given the ABC an opportunity to regain its strength as a unifying social force as Australians struggle to engage with a new normality. Rural and remote communities, tourists and city dwellers, have relied on its local radio emergency services and coverage of the bushfires, some for their lives. It is a great shame that, when its programming on radio and TV has responded so well to its role as a regional communicator, the economic crisis has prompted further budget cuts, further loss of valued staff from studios in Australia and around the world, and further loss of services. Since 2014 the ABC has lost $100 million a year in budget allocations.[4] Some of the most respected and longest serving public broadcasters and their programs have gone from our airwaves.

The government sector and those who, like the arts, depend on its funding, have suffered with the ABC the effects of economic policies that prioritise private sector growth over expenditure on the public good.

As traditional radio, television and film lost territory to social media, terrorists were among the earliest adopters of the new technology. They used it to recruit members and inform the world of their atrocities. In 2006 the federal Government announced its intention to reinvigorate the old sedition laws but, as so often in the past, the first casualty was not treason but satire, civil society's protection against government over-reach. In PP No.10, *Satire—or Sedition? The threat to national insecurity* Jonathan Biggins, actor, comedian, writer and creative member of the annual Wharf Revue, mounted a defence of free speech.

> *Within days of the Bill's introduction, a broad coalition of artists, performers, journalists, publishers and civil libertarians condemned the proposed laws as a threat to free speech. Why, they asked, were the existing sedition laws, last used in this country in the early 1960s, and effectively defunct ever since, being revitalised at this time when practically every other Western democracy had removed the crime of sedition from their statutes?* PP51, p.52

Biggins' Paper gives a history of the Sydney Theatre Company's annual Wharf Revue since its launch in 2000 and includes a Faustian dialogue in mock-Elizabethan verse, in which a fictional Philip Ruddock, an apparently dutiful but minor cabinet minister, makes a pact with the Devil (Nick Minchin, then Minister for Finance and Administration) for a term in the portfolio of Attorney General. When Minchin comes for his soul, Ruddock escapes damnation by claiming that the contract he signed in blood is 'open to interpretation' and his soul was only leased.[5]

> *So wily Ruddock to his word was true*
> *And stood with Reith as truth went overboard.*
> *In Tampa's wake he steered his Party through,*
> *His place beside his matter now assured.*
> *The borders shut, as iron walls descended*

Against poor souls left stateless and adrift.
Unburdened by his soul he now ascended,
Unshaken by a public family rift.
The eyes that once on tenderness reflected,
Now blankly lizard-like unblinking stared.
Incompetence concealed went undetected
While lawyer's tongue lashed anyone who cared.
PP10, p.48

National laws of sedition and censorship limited law-abiding printers and publishers, but did little to rein in anonymous destructive assaults launched from the international no man's land of the internet; and the regulatory confusion had other systemic effects.

In PP No.12, *Film in the Age of Digital Distribution* (2007) Richard Harris bravely navigated a course through the problems it was causing for film distributors. The introduction of multiple platforms added new layers of complexity for the distribution of films to exhibition houses. While recognising the opportunities they offered, Harris, who subsequently became executive director of the Australian Screen Directors' Association, warned that the industry should not lose sight of the value of its traditional broadcasting rights:

As we look to the options, it is important to keep in mind that while this new media landscape is opening up the conventional media world will continue to dominate. Furthermore, these broadcasters will still require access to spectrum, which will remain

> *a valuable public resource. In other words, while strategies for future media need to be developed, broadcasting regulations will remain as relevant as ever and need to be modified and augmented.*
> PP12, p.58

By 2013 the familiar paths to success, particularly for the local film industry had broken down, and, according to Lauren Carroll Harris in PP No.37, *Not at a Cinema Near You: Australia's film distribution problem*, distribution had succumbed to the effects Richard Harris had foreseen.

Economics, Cultural Policy and Government Funding

The internet transformed our culture, but it was a change in taxation law in 2000 that had the most profound effect on the arts. The introduction of the Australian Business Number (ABN) turned artists into 'small business owners'. No longer objects of patronage, they were free to trade in their own name, and their daily practices became the business activities of budding entrepreneurs.

In the years that followed, artists developed inter-disciplinary practices that merged the interpretive and authorial roles of actors, directors and writers in collaboration. However, as time went on, the adoption of corporate measures such as the key performance indicator (KPI) made funding agencies increasingly more of a hindrance than a help. Funding the arts requires a set of criteria, but the combination of old funding categories based on genre and company size, mixed with business measures, such as audience 'reach', placed obstacles in the way of innovation.

At the start of our Papers, in 2004, Christopher Latham, violinist and music festival director, wrote in PP No.2, *Survival of the Fittest: The artist versus the corporate world*, that making art had become an act of market competition:

> *The last thirty years have seen management displace the creators to become the powerful figures of the arts world. [...] Increasingly, even the section of artistic talent has been seen slipping from the hands of the sector towards the marketing and sponsorship departments [...] Australia needs its artists to initiate change, to rethink the present in the light of the past and begin to invest in a body of work that will in turn become their legacy.* PP2, p.12 *passim*

The use of business language was also causing a kind of social amnesia in the arts. It was making us forget the history of how we had come to do what we do and what we value among our achievements. Julian Meyrick, director and academic, described a theatre sector that was unable to incorporate the legacy of the past into its work in the present because it was at odds with its history.

In PP No.3, *Trapped by the Past: Why our theatre is facing paralysis*, he argued that the 'modern repertoire had been adapted to accommodate the philanthropy of the corporate world. Although some plays from the past were being revived with respectful performances, the productions displayed little knowledge of the conventions of the author's time or background'.

> *I have briefly described how this tradition played out in the unique soil of Australia; how it was transformed in the 1970s into a wholly distinctive mode of dramatic production; how inter-generational understanding between different practitioners was lost; and how we are today headed for exactly the same kind of impasse. What I have been working towards is the idea of wholeness—that artists working in Australian theatre are connected by myriad invisible wires, and each of these sings with specific, but nevertheless, shared, experience.* PP3, p.52

In PP No.4, *The Myth of the Mainstream: Politics and the performing arts in Australia today* (2005), cultural activist Robyn Archer proposed that modern marketing had sold the idea to the Australian public that its culture was homogenous. Whether the subject was race, sex or music, the 'mainstream' had its opinion. As a result, public commentary was losing its critical edge. It was important, she argued, for the press to distinguish between entertainment and intellectual challenge.

In 2005 it was hard to find an author brave enough to write about the Australia Council, which was becoming the subject of dissension. Confidence was at a low ebb and artists were reluctant to bite the hand that fed them. Keith Gallasch took up the challenge with PP No.6, *Art in a Cold Climate: Rethinking the Australia Council.* As the founding co-editor, with Virginia Baxter, of the journal *RealTime,* he had fought to retain informed critical writing on the arts. Gallasch's mood reflected the rage and gloom felt in the sector over the decline in public respect for the arts. In December 2000, without warning or consultation the Australia Council had announced a restructure that would include shutting down the New Media Arts Board. What conditions, what public attitudes, had compelled this decision? he asked:

> *Like the universities, like industry—and like them, through research and innovation—the arts have a responsibility to a future Australia. Have we become complacent at all levels about our capacity to invent?* PP4, p.38

The authors of Platform Papers so far had shown that artists could explain what was going wrong in their own particular sectors, but they found it much harder to mount a general defence of the arts. It was becoming increasingly apparent that the diverse values they were defending carried little weight separately and required a cultural policy to protect them. To date we still have only one such document, *Creative Nation,* initiated by Prime Minister Paul Keating in 1994.

In 2006 David Throsby, with PP No.7, *Does Australia Need a Cultural Policy?* outlined an approach to legislation that would provide criteria for measuring social and economic value. He pointed to the way our culture is embedded in the country's social and economic policies, and advised that our cultural values should be recognised in legislation at every level of government. Legislation is either top down or bottom up, he wrote, and in the case of culture he opted for bottom up.

> *A cultural policy is not a single document or statement or piece of legislation. It is the collection of actions that the government takes to create the conditions under which our cultural values, and indeed our whole cultural life, can find their expression. I have suggested that at the present moment in Australia's development we need a re-evaluation of what constitutes our cultural policy in this broad, all-embracing sense. I have drawn attention to some of the conflicting messages that bring about the need.* PP7, p.46

He also asked why Australia had abstained from voting on a UNESCO draft Universal Declaration on Cultural Diversity, which in 2005 had

> *focused worldwide attention on the importance of culture as an expression of fundamental human values [...] and elevated the role that cultural policy can, and should, play in national and*

> *international policy. Of the 154 delegates, 148 had voted in favour. The US and Israel voted against.*
>
> *[…] Why did we take such a conspicuously oppositional stand in an international arena where the diplomatic implications of voting behaviour do not go unnoticed? It is tempting to read Australia's abstention as simply another gesture of support for our great and powerful ally, and indeed this is exactly how it was interpreted. The official explanation, however, is based on technicalities, including concern that some aspects of the convention might conflict with our domestic policies.* PP7, pp.30–31

Throsby listed the conflicting messages coming from the Howard Cabinet at that time and suggested that we should begin by defining what we meant by culture and believed our culture to be.

Since publication, the arguments have continued. Throsby's Paper makes a valuable guide for anyone strong enough to take up the challenge of defining our cultural policy. In 2018, we asked if the climate was yet right for a new attempt. He returned to the question, and in the course of writing PP No.55, *Art, Politics, Money: Revising Australia's cultural policy*, reluctantly came to the conclusion that the answer was 'no'.

***

Choreographer Amanda Card was the first of our authors to point to the gaps in the Australia Council's project funding regulations, with PP No.8: *Body for Hire? The state of dance in Australia* (2006). Traditionally, dance had been hierarchical: choreographers dictated the movements and dancers were 'bodies for hire'. Now, in 2006, more collaborative forms of dance were emerging and Australia was at the forefront, but the Australia Council's 'Organisation Program' was not making life any more secure for small companies:

> *A case in point is De Quincey Co. Over the past six years the Sydney-based organisation, headed by Tess De Quincy, has 'enjoyed' an erratic and potentially fatal engagement with the Australia Council category. The company was granted Key Organisation Program funding in 2002, but not 2003. They were back on the list in 2004, but off again in 2005. This funding category should offer small organisations relief from the continuous merry-go-round of applications and recipients assume (rightly so) that it gives vital support to develop a small infrastructure to sustain the company.* PP8, p.17

In a mixture of excitement, over the renewal that had been achieved in modern dance by Australia Council funding in the 1980s, and exasperation at the lack of understanding that she saw as having undermined its progress since, Card called for a new system: a new way of employing choreographers and a better deal for dancers to re-invigorate dance once again.

Five years later Erin Brannigan, in PP No.25, *Moving Across Disciplines: Dance in the twenty-first century,* recorded the breakup of the old hierarchical relationship between the choreographer and the dancer; and in 2019 Sue Healey in PP No.60, *Capturing the Vanishing: A choreographer and film,* described a new way of escape—by embracing film. Dancefilm had opened a new career for her as a combined choreographer and photographer which has given her the independence to develop her work and enabled her dancers to be seen around the globe.

***

Despite some wins and a sustained period of economic growth, the arts were still not flourishing. In the search for an answer, the idea of building 'creative industries' was raised. In PP No.9, *What Price a Creative Economy?* (2006), Stuart Cunningham made a case for adopting the language of business and economics to frame the humanities, as a way of valuing the creative sector. However, if anything, this exercise served only to demonstrate how difficult—and disheartening—it was to harness culture's 'intrinsic' value to commercial gain. Artists were brought in on business and scholarly ventures, to add their insights to research, but while their skills provided *éclat* and style, the promised key to innovation eluded them. The concept struggled on for a decade and died of natural causes.

Lyndon Terracini, meanwhile, was turning the focus on the artist in the community. He had made his operatic career as a baritone in Europe before settling in Lismore in 1988. As the founding director of the Northern Rivers Performing Arts (NORPA), he had championed the commissioning and production of new operatic works in regional New South Wales; and, as director of the Queensland Music Festival 2000–05, mounted and locally produced popular music, dance and comedy shows with community performers, in small towns around the state. In PP No.11, *A Regional State of Mind: Making art outside metropolitan Australia* (2007), he argued for the need to make and create art in our own backyard:

> *...a reassessment of our perceived view of the relationship between amateur and professional organisations is needed. We need to look at the rough origins of our theatre and where we have taken it in the last thirty years. Then we might begin to see with new insight and different criteria, the store of energy contained in life outside our capitals. We might begin to acquire a regional state of mind.* PP11, p.33

Sadly, when he was appointed artistic director of Opera Australia two years later, his 'music of place' was not an element of his new administration.

The division between big and small had become irreconcilable and artists were searching for financial arguments for their defence. Academics Kay Ferres and David Adair quantified the contribution of the arts to the national economy. In PP No.14, *Who Profits from the Arts*? (2007) the authors traced the intricate social and financial connections between our cities' entertainment quarters and the theatres within them, for a project funded by the Australia Council. In PP No.15, *A Sustainable Arts Sector? What will it take?* (2008), Cathy Hunt and Phyllida Shaw, two arts strategists, followed with a collaborative plan for arts subsidy involving the public and private sectors. Hunt, with her company Positive Solutions, has since enabled extensive government support for community arts activity in regional Queensland.

Also in 2008 jazz guru Peter Rechnievski analysed the problems in the jazz scene, which, for all its apparent economic success, was delivering to musicians only the barest of livings. His PP No.16, *The Permanent Underground: Australian contemporary jazz in the new millennium* supported a boost to the creation of a national collective of jazz artists and audience.

National identity has always been a part of the Australia Council's remit. In PP No.17, *What is an Australian Play? Have we failed our ethnic writers?* (2008), Chris Mead asked how this intent should be defined by the funding regulators:

> *Australia has a turbulent present with a fragmented, hybrid population that continually renegotiates theorists' attempts to analyse them via class or post-colonialism. Xenophobia, distance, charity, religious freedom, migration, a rich land and a diverse people—all these combine to make*

> *Australia an extraordinary culture. But how much of that turbulence or difference reaches our stages?*
> PP17, p.6

At the end of 2008, with PP No.18, *Getting Heard: Achieving an effective arts advocacy*, former Shadow Arts Minister, Chris Puplick, closed the debate, advising artists that they must build unity of purpose within the sector before they could effectively lobby government for support. Groups who achieved an appointment with the Minister would find that time and attention was limited and applicants must be ready to speak briefly, cogently and with one voice—and leave a summary behind. Today this advice remains good.

***

2007 had seen the end of the Howard Government years in a landslide victory for the ALP under Kevin Rudd. Rudd began his term in office by convening the '2020 Summit' of experts, to construct a long-term, bi-partisan, strategy for the nation's future. 2008 found us in a fever of reform: Australia signed the Kyoto Protocol on climate change, drew up an emissions trading scheme, delivered a National Apology to the Stolen Generation, and introduced stimuli like the Education Revolution, funding new buildings; and a home insulation scheme, which faltered after a series of accidents, but all this was overshadowed by the global financial crisis. Rudd went out on a limb, spent $500billion on stimulus; and Australia survived without a recession. Despite these early successes, internal pressures split the party in 2010, resulting in a 'coup' in which Julia Gillard became Australia's first female prime minister.

In 2009 we turned attention again to the big picture and published PP No.19, *'Your Genre is Black': Indigenous performing arts policy.* Hilary Glow and Katya Johanson, with 18 Indigenous artists and advisers, gave the first hint of a solution to the fragmenting values that were plaguing arts policy. Aboriginal companies and creative artists had a myriad of problems, but the authors found their way through to devise a new beginning. Citing the theatre director David Milroy, they began with the basic principle that, among Aboriginal companies, the work of 'the arts', was integral to cultural and social policy:

> *Those who contribute to this policy debate might consider, as a starting point, the following questions:*
>
> 1. *Is the purpose of funding Indigenous performing arts to support cultural maintenance, or is it to encourage new and innovative work to emerge?*
> 2. *Who are (or should be) the audience for indigenous performing arts? Should the work be principally for Indigenous audiences, or should the work be enabled to reach mainstream audiences? If the latter is important, then how do we develop policy that will facilitate this?*
> 3. *Might the [proposed] National Indigenous Theatre Company swallow up scarce*

> *resources and marginalise the work of state-based Indigenous organisations? Or could a national flagship organisation dedicated to producing mainstage Indigenous work provide much-needed professional development and touring opportunities?* PP19, pp.58–60

Although the debate continues today, the States now have a variety of independent Indigenous performance companies of a high standard and community focus.

Christopher Sainsbury found these same problems in the music world ten years later and addressed them in PP No.59, *Ngarra-Burria: New music and the search for an Australian sound* (2019). He was brought up in Canberra in comfortable circumstances, and teaches at the ANU School of Music. When we invited him to write a Paper about Indigenous music and musicians in the field of contemporary (new) music we were both unaware of the emotions the decision would uncover. Sainsbury is a Dharug man from Sydney and has never denied his identity; but when he opened the conversation with others during the writing of his paper, he found himself plunged into a clamour of high emotion over clan identity and the appropriation of Indigenous folk music by white Australians. He described his meeting with Peter Sculthorpe:

> *'Do you know any Aboriginal composers?' I asked. He didn't. I then confided my Aboriginality,*

> *confident that, given his history of referencing Aboriginal music materials and concepts, themes and narratives in his works, that we would have an enjoyable conversation. I assumed that he would understand the importance to me of my heritage and identity. But he simply replied: 'Really? You don't look it.' I was shocked. Whilst it was dismissive, I don't believe it was intended to be rude.* PP59, p.15

Sainsbury stayed on track and drew attention in his Paper to his Ngarra-Burria, First People's Composers Program, whose concerts are making serious progress in uncovering a rich Australian orchestral sound.

While pressures on the arts have polarised opinion in the wider sector, Aboriginal artists have spoken with an increasingly unified voice, by connecting their art to their culture. This is a model that the arts as a whole would be well advised to emulate.

***

The fragmenting effect of market competition on the arts has been nowhere more apparent than in our major companies and educational institutions. One important initiative was the Actors' Company, a personal ambition of artistic director Robyn Nevin. Negotiations with the NSW Premier Bob Carr to establish a permanent ensemble of twelve actors at the Sydney Theatre Company had been going on since 1999. The aim had been to start the venture in 2005; but that time passed and Nevin put the project behind her.

When Carr announced the funding unexpectedly in 2006, she and the Company were caught unprepared for the task of integrating their intended experimental work into the busy timetable of a major theatre company. 'The complexity of it all was almost unbearable,' Nevin told James Waites for PP No.23, *Whatever Happened to the STC Actors' Company?* in 2010.[6] Between 2006 and 2009 the ensemble achieved some remarkable performances, in particular of Patrick White's *The Season at Sarsaparilla*, referencing the TV show *Big Brother*, a production that brought national attention also to the director Benedict Andrews. But despite these successes the Actors' Company never recovered from Carr's impulsive act.

Artists sweat out their lives to make their ventures look easy. When those who fund them are seduced into believing that their achievements happen 'by magic', opportunities are lost in the black hole of doomed hope.

A more knowing kind of maladministration was documented by Chris Puplick in PP No.33, *Changing Times at NIDA* (2012). The School's architects, John Clark and Elizabeth Butcher, were iconic figures in the industry. They had been its guide since 1969 and had built a great school, engineered the development and management of an enormous complex of buildings on the University of NSW campus, and had delivered fine performers, designers and technicians for over forty years.

Clark retired in 2004. When Butcher followed in 2008, Puplick wrote, the past four years were 'littered with the remnants of shattered members of staff, collegiality sacrificed on the altar of corporatism.'[7] The collapse of the family atmosphere that had been at the heart of the institution's culture was on full display in the Chairman's Report:

> *Her departure was recorded in that year's Annual Report by a mere fourteen words in the Chairman's Report and addition of her name to the names of five other departing staff in the Director's Report. No photo of Butcher was included and no attempt was made to recognise her forty years of incomparable service.* PP33, p.22

In 2004, Clark had been succeeded by Aubrey Mellor. When he retired, competition for the position of head of Australia's national theatre and TV school was high. The Australian list of applicants was formidable and the outcome unaccountable. Lynne Williams, an arts administrator from the UK, had little experience as a creative practitioner in the professional theatre; and only a modicum as a teacher.[8] Her tenure only deepened the crisis in management. When she resigned, no replacement was waiting in the wings. In October 2016 the theatre director Kate Cherry accepted the post, but she too left after only two years. NIDA's decline under changing hands is a familiar story and a credit to no-one, just another loss to Australia of a valued creative asset.

In 2014 music Professor Peter Tregear put his case for

bringing tertiary music qualifications into the modern world in PP No.38, *Enlightenment or Entitlement? Rethinking tertiary music education.* In 2012 he had taken on the task of moving the Canberra School of Music onto the Australian National University campus and with it a change of name and curriculum. Tertiary music, he wrote, was commonly thought of as preparing students for performance, but this conception had failed to address the shift in the ways most of us encounter music today. The failure to recognise the ubiquity of recorded music had led to a crisis in the sector that needed to be addressed, not by reducing performance tuition but by opening the students' minds to the new opportunities for performance and employment on offer today.

The Canberra School, now the ANU School of Music, was a revered institution and the prospect of change caused public outcry. In 2020 he wrote an account of the period, at the centre of which was a 'School of Music Implementation Plan' which had been delivered to him by the Vice Chancellor on his arrival and detailed a process by which the number of full-time-equivalent academic staff was to be reduced from 23.9 to 13 and professional staff from 9.23 to 7.5.

> *This may explain, at least in part, why the ANU's management of the School of Music, alongside a number of other prominent discipline-centred controversies in recent years, have caused it so much grief. Changes it imposed on the School appeared*

> *to many to have been motivated by managerial priorities that seemed at best indifferent not only to the particular traditions and needs of music scholarship, but also to this discipline's capacity to contribute to the public mission of a university more generally.*[9]

A year after he left, exhausted, in 2015, a review found 'a climate of distrust, emotional stress, poor management and falling standards' within the school.[10] Tregear returned to a teaching fellowship at Royal Holloway, University of London. He is now Dean of St Mark's College, Adelaide, and works between Australia and Europe as a singer, conductor and writer. He was replaced in 2017 by Professor Ken Lampl, a Julliard School graduate, who planned to set up a course in musical composition for film, television and video gaming. He too resigned, in 2019. The School has now embarked on a new life of contemporary musicianship under the care of the eclectic musician and composer Kim Cunio. Despite the Covid-19 pandemic, enrolments have risen.

We saw in Chris Puplick's account of NIDA's overhaul how painful the change to, or interference with, an embedded culture can be; and how it may defy the best arguments. Creators, particularly, are damaged by change or exclusion because their whole personality is engaged with the act of creation. That is why, to so many, the disappearance of Canberra's revered School of Music had been so contentious.

***

In 2013, Leigh Tabrett, former Deputy-Director General of the Department of Premier and Cabinet and Head of Arts Queensland from 2003–12, offered an insider's view of the decision-making processes of well-intentioned parliamentarians and their departmental heads, who 'didn't know what they didn't know'.

During her time as a public servant, Tabrett had led a complete reorganisation of Arts Queensland and supervised the refurbishment of the Queensland Performing Arts Centre. Following retirement, she gave us in PP No.34, *It's Culture, Stupid! Reflections of an arts bureaucrat* (2013), an entertaining account of those years. More importantly, she revealed the many pitfalls of the subsidy system that awaited parliamentarians and other innocents with too-little knowledge of arts practice, and artists who lacked the business head to recognise the dilemma.

> *A question which Arts Ministers sometimes ask is: 'Why do we keep giving money to the same people year after year? When are they going to be able to stand on their own two feet so we can give someone else a turn?'* PP34, p.23

Tabrett concluded her Paper more soberly by setting out seven actions that could help both sides reach a better understanding. There followed a proposal for a nationally agreed statement on the importance of culture and the purpose of public investment in it—something deserving wider attention.

In the 1970s Brisbane's long-established pro-am culture boycotted the State Government's attempts to impose a state theatre. Today Queensland has buried the memories of this notorious decade and South Brisbane has a famous cultural precinct and theatre complex of which the city is justly proud. But the old wicked problems of measuring cultural value, or of any publicly-funded project surviving the term of a single government, are still hurdles to be overcome.

That same year David Pledger produced one of our most passionately argued papers, PP No.36, *Re-valuing the Artist in the New World Order* (2013). Pledger is a leading creator, producer, writer and thinker on the value of artists to society. At a time when our last attempt to achieve a cultural policy had been shelved by yet another election, he gave sober advice on the danger of losing the arts. Artists, he wrote, were integral to making sense of our changing global landscape. They were society's antennae, the canaries in the coalmine of global change.

> *In short, if you want to know where you will be in twenty years, follow an artist. If you want to get there before everyone else, fund them.* PP36, p.26

Nations and societies that understand this today, writes Pledger, would be more culturally, socially, environmentally and economically viable.

***

In PP No.39: *The Retreat of our National Drama* (2014), Julian Meyrick called for a better research culture to revive, with deeper understanding, the past history of Australian playwriting. The work-shopping of texts has become regular practice, but, at that time, the immediate outcomes were proving disappointing. In the major companies, the time for experiment had been reduced and was being regulated by the demands of the subscription season. But in the so called 'small to medium' sector, companies, writers and directors were finding their own way.

As with the ANU School of Music, the artists coming to prominence were starting to challenge an outdated performance industry and imposing change with action. The sudden prevalence of deconstructed European classics on stage in Sydney was a symptom of a new and very personal exploration of text and performance by our senior directors and actors. These free interpretations of the classics created a furore in the media. 'What on earth is going on?' asked Meyrick.

In retrospect, what was going on was a period of maturation, for which the infrastructure of the arts was unprepared. In this thoughtful study Meyrick detailed the intentions that had brought it about and made the practical suggestion that we establish a collaborative national theatre workshop to grapple with this challenge of self-assertion.

Productive collaboration, however, was not in the air. Without warning, the Arts Minister, George Brandis, attempted to do away with the troublesome 'small to medium' sector altogether by diverting support to a fund under the Minister's direct control. Ben Eltham's PP

No.48, *When the Goal Posts Move* (2016), was a towering piece of research into the extraordinary circumstances of the 'excellence raid' on Budget night, Friday 13 May 2015, which left the entire arts sector unprepared and helpless.

'The result was a bloodbath', he wrote: '65 organisations were defunded and more than a hundred that applied were also unsuccessful. The arts sector dubbed it Black Friday.'

> *Some of the most famous arts companies in the country missed out [...] The defunding of a slew of Australia's best-known smaller arts companies was due to a decision made by the Abbott Government Arts Minister George Brandis, who had taken $105million in funding from the Australia Council a year before. Funding cuts bit deep. The decision came in addition to $87million slashed from the Arts portfolio in 2014. Further cuts of $52.5million were handed down in December 2015. All told, according to the Australian Labor Party's Mark Dreyfus, approximately $300million had been cut from federal cultural funding by the Coalition.* PP48, pp.1–2

The impact of the federal cutback affected all aspects of the subsidised arts, not least the Australia Council itself. It was widely thought that it would not survive and conversation began to turn to what would happen next. The cuts had done immense damage to the Council's reputation in the industry as an independent 'arm's length' agency of government. The longer-term effects are still playing out today.

The other three Papers for 2015 were similarly directed at how to put things right by clarifying the purpose of funding the arts. My own, No. 43, *The Arts and the Common Good*, showed how decisions made at the start of subsidy had bred distrust between the arts sector and government; and how social policy had been buried under the endless tussles between the two. PP No.44, by Justin Macdonnell, *Cultural Precincts: Art or commodity?* examines the role of the long outdated distinction between 'high' and 'commercial' art in the Government's thinking; and in PP No.45: *Paying the Piper: There has to be another way*, Cathy Hunt exposes the fragility of a nation's arts funding brought down by an overnight change of Prime Minister and Cabinet; and puts forward a case for a new financial framework that draws on both government and private investment.

Justin O'Connor's PP No.47, *After the Creative Industries: Why we need a cultural economy* (2016), examines how the value of the arts has been tested through history. In the 1980s prosperity and creativity in Australia had combined in an intoxicating mix that ended with the stock market crash of 1987, after which the arts turned to the market to be its judge and saviour. O'Connor follows the rise and fall of the creative industries experiment and asserts the need for a reinvigorated cultural economy. 'What is at stake in culture', he concludes,

> *as has always been, though we frequently forget it, are the great questions of ultimate value: of how we can live together and what the quality of our collective experience should be. These have not disappeared in an age of cultural abundance. They are even more urgent, as the possibility of a truly human creative society is in one way more realisable, in another as far away as it has ever been.* PP47, pp.57–8

These last years had been drawing the arts closer and closer to the demands of the business world. In No.41, *Education and the Arts: Creativity in the promised new order* (2014), Meg Upton and Naomi Edwards dissected a new threat to the arts in the form of the Australian Curriculum, aimed at nationalising secondary education, previously the responsibility of the states. This new nationally endorsed secondary-school curriculum emphasised science, technology, engineering and mathematics (STEM) as essential subjects, while the arts and humanities were elective. This reform, to put the best face on it, was probably not intended to class the humanities as dispensable but to meet the Government's priority to raise employment—the key to which, it was assumed, lay in 'practical' subjects, not the abstract contemplations of the arts and humanities. When times are tough there's no room for imagination.

The Global Stage

Another effect of the internet was globalisation. Australian artists have a long history of leaving the country to pursue their careers. The internet did not change this trend, but it has produced a more cosmopolitan outlook. Back in 2005, in PP No.5, *Shooting Through: Australian Film and the Brain Drain*, filmmaker Storry Walton had discussed the relationship between Australian artists and the global stage:

> *We have always felt ambivalent about the idea of ships and planes bearing away our talent. It has betokened a fear of the loss of native imagination, or worse, natural intelligence. It has signified regret and guilt—regret at losing our brightest and guilt at not being able to keep them. It has meant pride in their achievement and disdain, should they return without accolades—'They weren't really good enough, you know.'* PP5, p.4

This fear of 'not being good enough' is familiar to older Australians and in 2005, despite government's encouragement since the 1960s, it was still hard for filmmakers to make a living here. Walton's proposed solution was to fund a program of 'sabbaticals' to encourage expatriate artists to return home to work.

However, the world was rapidly becoming a much smaller place and the parochial idea of the 'expat' has fallen out of use. Today many of our film and stage artists, concert musicians, visual artists and academics, have built their reputations overseas. They see themselves as part of a world community; and they return to Australia between jobs, because this is where they are at home.

Theatre director Neil Armfield got his start as co-director of the Nimrod Theatre in 1979, and in 1994 became the founding artistic director of its successor, the Belvoir Street Theatre Company, in its present premises. Now in his 60s, he spends most time directing opera in the UK and Europe but keeps his base in Sydney. Benedict Andrews, twenty years younger, first came to national attention at the Sydney Theatre Company in 2009 for his massive two-part adaptation of Shakespeare's history plays, under the title *The War of the Roses.* He also applied his talent to authors like Tennessee Williams, including a famous *A Streetcar Named Desire.* He now lives in Reykjavic and works throughout Europe and the US, directing opera, film and classic drama.

Barrie Kosky, born and raised in Melbourne of European Jewish parentage, has shared an ambivalent relationship with his native land. His Australian career has been a continuing source of controversy. In his twenties he made his mark as artistic director of a spectacular 1996 Adelaide Festival, after which he made his home in Europe, firstly at the Vienna Schauspielhaus. He is now among the first rank of directors in the northern hemisphere. His international reputation rests mainly on opera and includes work at the Bayreuth, Frankfurt, Glyndebourne and Los Angeles opera houses. The catalogue of his work in Europe is prodigious—all but a fraction are opera classics.

The director Simon Stone, still in his 30s, lives where the work is. He was born of Australian parents in Basel, Switzerland, and grew up in Melbourne and Cambridge. In 2007 he founded the Hayloft Project in Melbourne, and later transferred to the Belvoir Street Theatre. His adaptation of Ibsen's *The Wild Duck*, staged inside a Perspex box, was the cause of both admiration and scandal in Sydney for its startling Australian reinterpretation of Ibsen's characters. In 2015 he returned to Europe and now works mainly in Amsterdam.

It will not have escaped the reader's notice that these directors are all male. Our female directors have had a tougher journey; but two who stand out on their own terms are Gale Edwards and Lindy Hume.

Edwards began her career in Adelaide with the youth theatre Energy Connection; and directed for the state theatre companies until she moved to London in the 1990s. In 1996 she directed the London revival of *Jesus Christ Superstar*, which transferred to Broadway in 2000, and won an Emmy award for the television production. Since then she has directed for the Royal Shakespeare Company and the Shakespeare Theatre Company in Washington, DC; and in 2003 she directed the premiere in Sydney of the musical *The Boy from* Oz and Sondheim's *Sweeney Todd,* for which she received Helpmann awards.

Lindy Hume has for years travelled the globe directing opera. From 1992 to 1996 she was director of the

Western Australian Opera; then of the Victorian Opera from 2004 to 2007 and thereafter the Perth and Sydney festivals to 2012. In 2004 she chose to settle on the south coast of New South Wales and join the community of artists gathering there. In PP No.50, *Restless Giant: Changing cultural values in regional Australia*, she described her way of life and how she had made the leap from one reality to another:

> *In the decade since [coming here], regional Australia has been a constant inspiration and focus. Coming home to the beautiful South Coast and my local community has sustained me, grounded me, providing aesthetic inspiration, a sanctuary for reflection. Community values have informed my work and identity as Festival Director of Sydney Festival and Artistic Director of Opera Queensland, and as a freelance director in Australia, Europe, New Zealand and America.* PP50, p.4

Government has also encouraged Australians to expand their careers by going abroad. In 2012 veteran Asia-watchers Alison Carroll and Carrillo Gantner examined the strategy of 'soft diplomacy' employed by the Department of Foreign Affairs and Trade in PP No.31, *Finding a Place on the Asian Stage*. Funding stars like Cate Blanchett to tour an Australian production of a world classic, they argued, might be good for government kudos but did little for trade relations. They proposed instead the creation of an Australian

International Cultural Agency to oversee policy, programs and funding. Its responsibilities would include not only art and performance but international education, public festivals and events, collaborations, the establishment of cultural centres in major cities and programs directed towards the international exchange of talent and knowledge.

This paper did not bring the kind of thoughtful response it deserved. Cultural policy was not top of mind in Canberra at that moment. Politics had become personal and vindictive following the dramatic 'coup' that saw Kevin Rudd replaced by Julia Gillard. Gillard, in turn, fell victim to factional in-fighting in a series of leadership spills. The extraordinary abuse on social media to which she was subjected shone a spotlight on the 'trolling' endured by women in the public domain, but was eclipsed by her 'misogyny speech', addressed to Opposition Leader Tony Abbott, in 2012.[11] In 2013 she lost office and retired, unbroken and visibly unscathed; and has continued to contribute skilfully to public policy and life. But it was an ugly, exhausting period, full of auguries. Since the election in 2016 of Donald Trump as President of the United States, Australia's foreign affairs in Asia have been dominated by America's rivalry with China.

***

Artists were also drawn abroad by commercial success. The entrepreneurial spirit, fostered by the economic changes, policy reforms and technological advances since 2000, found its outlet in a wave of musical and dance theatre. Australians are good at music and dance shows: at performing them and attending them. The Bangarra Dance Theatre has won a national award almost annually since its founding in 1991; and shows like *Bran Nue Dae* (1990), *Tap Dogs* (1995) and *The Boy from Oz* (1998), were home grown works that ran, and continued to run, in Australia and overseas for years. This was only the beginning.

A key figure in this efflorescence was the dynamic producer Baz Luhrmann, who gained national attention straight out of NIDA. Luhrmann's *Strictly Ballroom* began life as a student production at NIDA in 1984, played around Australia and then became a film. By 1992, his partnership with designer Catherine Martin was merging art, fashion and culture, to create the trademark style of their 'Red Curtain Trilogy': *Strictly Ballroom, William Shakespeare's Romeo + Juliet* (1996) and *Moulin Rouge* (2001). These films carried the theatrical sensibility of the stage onto the screen and around the world.

In 2009, Stephan Elliott and Alan Scott took the opposite direction, transforming the film of *Priscilla Queen of the Desert* into a stage show. It opened in Sydney in 2006, played London's West End in 2009, and continued to tour in Britain and the US until halted, like Tim Minchin's *Matilda* for the Royal Shakespeare Company, and P. J. Hogan, Kate Miller-Heidke and Keir Nuttal's *Murial's Wedding*, by the ubiquitous Covid-19 virus.

By 2016 the adventurous directors and designers of the 1990s were in their 50s, independent cosmopolitans who used the internet to make their connections. Their work spanned opera, musicals, dance, circus and drama that toured Europe and occasionally North America and Asia.

Musicals require an enormous infrastructure of space, equipment, skills and talent. In 2015, John Senczuk, an imaginative and versatile theatre-maker with a healthy respect for the business side of the arts, outlined a plan in PP No.42, *The Time is Ripe for the Great Australian Musical,* for creating our own musicals industry by pooling the resources of Australia's production companies. The timing of the publication was unlucky. It was February 2015 and three months later the Australia Council's expected funding was plundered for the next four years. Senczuk's plan attracted producers but in the uneasy climate was judged too risky. In 2020 many large shows around the world have been brought to a standstill by the pandemic, while others have converted risk into opportunity.

Hasty laws and political obstruction, risk aversion and embarrassment at commercial success, still dog Australian creative enterprise. There is such loneliness about the way we work in the arts. 2015 saw the death of many hopes for lack of that quality of generosity and collaboration of which we are so capable. Given the success of other endeavours, this outcome was disappointing.

***

Over 2016–17 we published a sub-series, *The Professionals*, which gave insight into what it had been like for individuals to live through the tumultuous changes we had been documenting for more than a decade. As with all the Papers, these were for me an illumination.

In PP No.46, *The Designer: Decorator or dramaturg?* Stephen Curtis describes how his work as a stage designer for a major theatre company requires agility to find visual expression for the words on the page and synthesis with the director and actors' own imagination. There had been a time when the designer was not on the payroll until all the production choices had been made; and was required to do no more than provide a picture frame for the production. Today his work is integrated and extensive. At the Sydney Theatre Company Curtis was drawn into Neil Armfield's creative team and in 2016 designed what became the much-applauded, emotionally-grounded bush setting of the play *The Secret River*, adapted by Andrew Bovell from the prize-winning novel by Kate Grenville.

In PP No.49, *The Lighting Designer: What is 'good' lighting?* Nigel Levings told how he began work at His Majesty's Theatre in Melbourne as a youth hired to keep the lights on. With each job he learned new skills until, by 2016, he was winning international awards and controlling giant digital lighting desks in the great theatres around the world. The best lighting, in his view, goes unnoticed but enables the characters on stage to be effectively seen to the back of the gallery. (Another kind of theatrical 'magic'.)

PP No.52 *Putting Words in Their Mouths: The playwright and screenwriter at work* (2017), was the work of the prolific stage and screen writer, Andrew Bovell. Bovell first made his mark in the spartan conditions of the Melbourne Workers' Theatre and has had notable stage and screen success, here and abroad, with plays like *After Dinner, Speaking in Tongues* (which became the film *Lantana*) and *When the Rain Stops Falling*. His recent plays have achieved a pattern of extended life in the UK, Europe and the USA; and he now spends much of his year working abroad. His recent family drama, *Things I know to be True,* has already been successful in the UK and America. His screenplays include *Strictly Ballroom, Edge of Darkness, Lantana* and *Head On.*

All these personal accounts of professional lives spent in the arts, tell stories of artistic survival. In PP No.53, *The Jobbing Actor: Rules of engagement*, Lex Marinos described what that means for actors:

> *How to define the jobbing actor? Not the handful who find fame and fortune and power. The ones that audiences pay to see. I want to write about the vast majority of actors, the ones that struggle to stay employed.* PP53, p.12

Marinos is Australian-born of Greek parents and has earned his living almost entirely in this country. In 1970 he was cast in the pantomime *Hamlet on Ice* at the fledgling Nimrod Street Theatre (now Griffin) and quickly crossed into radio and television at the

ABC. In the 1980s he spent four years playing the Italian-Australian character 'Bruno' in the TV comedy *Kingswood Country.*

> *I maintained that as he was born here he should speak with a normal Australian accent. I was sick of seeing, and playing, stereotypical 'wogs'—not that there were many then in our Anglo-centric television shows. The producers/writers agreed with me, and it proved a smart move.* PP53, p.30

Working in an unregulated industry takes a huge toll on the health of actors, both mental and physical, and Marinos has some advice on that. Acting schools have begun preparing their graduates for the challenges of life as jobbing actors. They are better trained than they have ever been, but it remains a precarious career:

> *Apart from their acting skills they will have also been trained in marketing and technology, financial planning and legal requirements, lifestyle and resilience skills. They will have a show reel, a voice tape and a five-year plan.[...] All will have just a year to establish themselves before the marketplace receives the next three hundred graduates.* PP53, p.66

The authors of *The Professionals* share one overwhelming characteristic: devotion to their work and a willingness to go to the limit every time. Levings says that the aim of the best lighting is to go unnoticed. The same can be said of the best acting, dancing and writing: the outcome, when it is good, appears effortless. That is the paradox of being a performer.

Mark Williams, a Melbourne lawyer with a long professional interest in the welfare of the creative sector, details the eccentric conditions under which performers work, and their irregular relationship to our health and welfare services, in PP No.56, *Falling Through the Gaps: Artists' health and welfare* (2018). These support systems have been upgraded or re-regulated at intervals, he explains, but at every turn the artist/performer has eluded the benefits. In the past, an actor who won a major role in a television series, and was required to be on call, could have expected a fulltime salary for the whole of the contract period. Today the practice of paying actors only for the hours they work can reduce the period of their employment on a major production to weeks or even a few days.

How is it fair that the spectacular global success of our entrepreneurs should be at the cost of the workers who star in them? These advances have been built on the invisible talents of our local jobbing artists. To be innovative, artists need the investment of government grants, but to survive and succeed they need a living wage.

3. Division and Cultural Unity

The first Platform Paper to gain mainstream media coverage was Lee Lewis' PP No.13, *Cross-Racial Casting: Changing the face of Australian Theatre* in 2007. She earned her MFA in Acting from Columbia University and worked as an actor and director in Manhattan before returning to Australia at a time when finding work depended more than ever on whom you knew. She had been unemployed for over a year when she confided to me one day that she was disturbed by the *whiteness* of the productions she had seen on stage since her return. Why did the casting not reflect the variety of faces she saw in the street? The outcome was the Paper she wrote for us. As expected, the media made a meal of her observations and Lewis faced the possibility of never working in the theatre again.

Seven years later, I asked her to reflect on her decision to speak out. She responded generously:

> *The Currency House Platform Paper I wrote was the hardest thing I have ever done and the best. Personally and professionally, the effort and the repercussions shaped my work and my career path in great and*

awful ways and I believe will continue to do so for the rest of my life. The commitment to the articulation of private observation in a public and permanent sphere both forced a clarity I had not faced before and courage I had not anticipated needing.

The reaction to the paper was severe and enlightening. It enabled me to meet a level of Australian thought makers and theatre makers in a new way and to form conversations which continue to this day. I had to learn how to speak the sentences I had written in the face of people who alternately opposed and celebrated the ideas. I met sides of people I had not wanted to realise existed. I was discussing institutional racism but encountered first-hand evidence of personal racism in embedded and unexpected places.

The paper keeps me in touch with my fierce younger self. Every day I am haunted by my ability to change the status quo or maintain it. The paper means I will never be able to let myself off the hook. It was written as a direct appeal to directors to acknowledge the difference they can make in shaping the visual and aural imagination of this country to long-term political effect. I am aware of every instance where I fail in my own productions to push the conversation further. As I get older I know more about why different decisions are made—why various casting decisions are made; why the cast you hoped for is not the cast you have. I go to bed at times knowing that while I have

> *made a good production I have failed my younger voice that says every production is an opportunity to change expectations. I understand the compromise process more, but I do not live with it well. I don't credit the paper with changing anything—words don't make change, actions inspired by those words do. I still look forward to the time when this paper is redundant.*[12]

Despite the reaction of the media, by the time Lewis's Paper was published she was directing at the Sydney Opera House. In 2012 she was appointed director of the Griffin Theatre and in 2019 artistic director of Queensland Theatre. Not immediately but, gradually, on stage and in film and television, brown and Asian faces began to take their place in the repertoire. Today their appearance in 'white' roles goes unremarked. This change has enabled fine actors like Deborah Mailman, Wayne Blair and Aaron Pedersen to take on the roles their skills merit and gain the admiration they deserve. They have made a difference and been awarded for it.

***

Not all the Papers we have published have received a mention in this essay. But all of them deserve repeated reading—for their motivation, their good advice and their determination to work for a better future in the face of a bleak outlook.

Since the Australia Council was established in 1968 to bring value and recognition to our arts workers, the arts have been weakened by strategies of divide and conquer: division into genres, major and minor arts organisations, and even the entrepreneurialism encouraged by the ABN, has pitted art forms, companies and individual artists against each other in competition for the arts dollar.

Wesley Enoch's PP No.40, *Take Me to Your Leader: The dilemma of cultural leadership* (2014), speaks for his fellow artists; and is compulsory reading for anyone trying to understand what has gone so wrong in the arts sector; how these curious gaps have appeared in our cultural understanding and what the consequences might be:

> *In the 1970s, with the establishment of the Australia Council, we saw the formalising of some kind of official culture. Funding provided a framework within which to experiment and explore ideas that examine Australian life and reflect our own aspirations. The question today is whether the idea of a state-sanctioned culture has led to the taming and silencing of the rambunctious dissenting mob that had ruled our performing arts for over two centuries. In the search for the approval of the public purse, have we lost our wit and charm, the art of surviving through persuasion, our critical purpose and our taste for the popular?* PP40, p.13

Public funding has divided the arts, and their defences have been systematically dismantled. The funding bodies' emphasis on art form has divided and narrowed the interests that artists hold in common. This has meant that problems have been discussed in terms of outcomes. The Australia Council's creation in 1999 of the Major Performing Arts Group (AMPAG) divided the territory between a privileged group of 28 established arts organisations and the 'small-to-medium' sector. This was a further separation between big and small, and was similarly interpreted as a division between those companies who would be supported to survive, and the rest. It was, of course, controversial from the start and it led inexorably to what must be the lowest point in the Arts/Government relationship: the moment when Minister Brandis siphoned off the money for the small to medium sector and AMPAG stayed silent. Despite their privilege, no-one was prepared to gamble their company's livelihood, or their own. Wesley Enoch names himself among them.[13] AMPAG has now been disbanded but the problem of indifference, between artists and the arts bureaucracy, remains manifest.

We need to find a way to unify without suppressing diversity. Artists need to see what they do as an expression of culture and society first, and as a product to be marketed second. We must turn back to our old strengths: bringing people together and allowing them to feel part of society by enjoying the pleasures of their culture.

The problems of the arts should be discussed in terms of what artists need for a productive life: sustained employment, health, advocacy, funding priorities and social recognition. Actors lost their most powerful industrial defence—the face of celebrity representing their rights—when in 1992 Actors' Equity merged with the Journalists' Association, to become the Media Alliance. Celebrity has been harnessed to promotion. Some essential work in the public sphere that Equity once did (or failed to do) has now been picked up by Theatre Network Australia.

The global crises we face at the moment are an opportunity to reposition the arts in relation to society and the economy. They have forced us to turn inwards—no international travel, no interstate travel, no crowds, the things that have fed economic growth and the rise of globalisation to date—and we have learned, 'We're all in this together'. At the highest level, research companies have joined forces to find a vaccine. Former competitors are sharing their resources. Ruthless market competition and self-reliant individualism will no longer serve.

It is easy to blame the regulators and to see the arts worker as an eccentric, vulnerable figure that public power and policy have failed. But the pattern I still see, after trudging through the stages of our history and watching how the fortunes of creative people have followed the money and its opportunities, is that from the outset the decision of the Australian Government to take responsibility for the arts sector was made under terms that were fatally flawed.

Maybe at the time the idea of an Australia Council for the Arts was just a welcome distraction for the baby-boomers who had reached their majority and were up for the Vietnam conscription ballot. Regulation was loose, arts practitioners welcomed the funding and the arts blossomed into the New Wave. In the first years of the Council its field officers were arts workers who travelled the country and became our mentors, quietly showing us how to design our project and fill in the application form. Then their travel was halted. Perhaps the cause was the oil crisis of the early 70s, but whatever the reason, within four years the bureaucrats were in charge. Vital initiatives were overruled by people with more clout, and gradually the needs of the patron and that of the artist, diverged. We who were observers and in a position to call for a rewind on the original criteria missed our chance

Nevertheless, the Australia Council has transformed civil society. Today we have arts institutions, performance and teaching facilities, theatres and concert halls to admire. Would they be here, had it been left to the private sector? Or would it have been done differently? By now, the creative sector should long ago have been written into social policy. It should have an Arts Minister and a Department staffed by arts workers, dedicated to forward planning and fostering collaborative enterprises: a Department like that proposed by Alison Carroll and Carrillo Gantner in PP No.31, *Finding a Place on the Asian Stage* (2012).

Instead of persisting in the endless, competitive pursuit of excellence, why not evaluate the needs of a healthy arts sector and set about putting them in place? Why not consider every one of the many innovative plans proposed by our authors over the past sixteen years that 'fall outside the guidelines'? A first step would be to change the language: define individual Australia Council grants, now seen as money with which to produce art, as money for cultural research.

Since 2000, artists have been too frightened to speak out in case they lose an elusive chance for work. Don't be afraid to say you are out of work. Today more than half the country is out of work; and rethinking their priorities. What have we got to lose?

Reforming the arts requires good advisers, good records, a collaborative strategy, funds to experiment and a living wage. My hope is that, as we come out of this dark period in our history, Australia might take the lead in the challenge to make the world a kinder, more inclusive place than it has been. By living too fast we have come too quickly to the end of the road. 'A Change for the Better' is the Platform Papers' motto. All we need is the courage to make it.

Endnotes

1 Harry Lime is a fictional American survivalist played by Orson Welles in the British film noir *The Third Man* (1949), written by Graham Greene, directed by Carol Reed, and set in a grim post-war Vienna. The Ferris-wheel conversation between Lime and his childhood friend Holly Martins (Joseph Cotton) is legendary in film history. In 1999 *The Third Man* was voted the greatest British film of all time by the British Film Institute.

2 John Howard, election speech, 28 October 2001, https://electionspeeches.moadoph.gov.au/speeches/2001-john-howard

3 Its name was changed to Australian Broadcasting Corporation under the Act of 1983, marking an important transition away from the culture of the BBC.

4 Amanda Meade, *Guardian* 4 May 2020 'ABC loses more than $783m funding since 2016 when Coalition made its first cuts – report' https://www.theguardian.com/media/2020/may/04/abc-loses-793m-funding-since-2014-when-coalition-made-its-first-cuts-report

5 'The Damnation of Ruddock' in Platform Papers 10, *Satire or Sedition? The threat to national insecurity*, 2005, pp.44–50.

6 PP33, p.4.

7 PP33, p.21.

8 PP33, p.16.

9 Peter Tregear, 'Time to face the Music?' *Demos Journal*, 31 January 2020, http://demosjournal.com/

time-to-face-the-music/

10 Emma Macdonald, 'Australian National University's School of Music 'poorly managed by the university at all levels'. *Canberra Times* 2 May 2016. Review by Public Commissioner Andrew Podger of the ANU School. https://www.canberratimes.com.au/story/6050121/australian-national-universitys-school-of-music-poorly-managed-by-the-university-at-all-levels/

11 Julia Gillard's speech at Question Time on 9 October 2012 began: 'I rise to oppose the motion moved by the Leader of the Opposition [Tony Abbott]. And in so doing I say to the Leader of the Opposition I will not be lectured about sexism and misogyny by this man. I will not. And the Government will not be lectured about sexism and misogyny by this man. Not now, not ever.' The speech was later declared the most watched speech on TV that year.

12 In the possession of the author.

13 PP40, p.29.

Appendix: Platform Papers, 2004–21

First published July 2004

PP1 *'Our ABC'—A Dying Culture?* Martin Harrison

PP2 *Survival of the Fittest: The artist versus the corporate world*, Christopher Latham

2005

PP3 *Trapped by the Past: Why our theatre is facing paralysis*, Julian Meyrick

PP4 *The Myth of the Mainstream: Politics and the performing arts in Australia today*, Robyn Archer

PP5 *Shooting Through: Australian film and the brain drain*, Storry Walton

PP6 *Art in a Cold Climate: Rethinking the Australia Council*, Keith Gallasch

2006

PP7 *Does Australia Need a Cultural Policy?* David Throsby

PP8 *Body for Hire? The state of dance in Australia*, Amanda Card

PP9 *What Price a Creative Economy?* Stuart Cunningham

PP10 *Satire—or Sedition? The threat to national insecurity*, Jonathan Biggins

2007

PP11 *A Regional State of Mind: Making art outside metropolitan Australia*, Lyndon Terracini

PP12 *Film in the Age of Digital Distribution: The challenge for Australian content*, Richard Harris

PP13 *Cross-racial Casting: Changing the face of Australian theatre*, Lee Lewis

PP14 *Who Profits from the Arts? Taking the measure of culture*, Kay Ferres and David Adair

2008

P15 *A Sustainable Arts Sector: What will it take?* Cathy Hunt and Phyllida Shaw

PP16 *The Permanent Underground: Australian contemporary jazz in the new Millennium*, Peter Rechniewski

PP17 *What is an Australian Play? Have we failed our ethnic writers?* Chris Mead

PP18 *Getting Heard: Achieving an effective arts advocacy*, Chris Puplick

2009

PP19 *'Your Genre is Black': Indigenous performing arts and policy* Hilary Glow and Katya Johanson

PP20 *Beethoven or Britney: The great divide in music education*, Robert Walker

PP21 *Television: What will rate in the new tomorrow?* Ian David

PP22 *Copyright, Collaboration and the future of dramatic authorship*, Brent Salter

2010 (one paper cancelled)

PP23 *Whatever Happened to the STC Actors Company?* James Waites

PP24 *The Digital Playing Fields: New rulz for film art and performance*, Shilo McClean

PP25 *Moving Across Disciplines: Dance in the twenty-first century*, Erin Brannigan

2011

PP26 *Not Just an Audience: Young people transforming our theatre*, Lenine Bourke and Mary Ann Hunter

PP27 *Hello, World! Promoting the arts on the web*, Robert Reid

PP28 *The Fall and Rise of the VCA*, Richard Murphet

PP29 *Democracy versus Creativity in Australian Classical Music*, Nicole Canham

2012

P30 *Indig-curious: Who can play Aboriginal roles?* Jane Harrison

PP31 *Finding a place on the Asian stage*, Alison Carroll and Carrillo Gantner

PP32 *History is Made at Night: Live music in Australia*, Clinton Walker

PP33 *Changing Times at NIDA*, Chris Puplick

2013

PP34 *It's Culture, Stupid! Reflections of an arts bureaucrat*, Leigh Tabrett

PP35 *The Music of Place: Reclaiming the practice*, Jon Rose

PP 36 *Re-valuing the Artist in the New World Order*, David Pledger

PP37 *Not at a Cinema Near You: Australia's film distribution problem*, Lauren Carroll Harris

2014

PP38 *Enlightenment or Entitlement? Rethinking tertiary music education*, Peter Tregear

PP39 *The Retreat of our National Drama*, Julian Meyrick

PP40 *Take Me to Your Leader: The dilemma of cultural leadership*, Wesley Enoch

PP41 *Education and the arts: Creativity in the promised new order*, Meg Upton with Naomi Edwards

2015

PP42 *The Time Is Ripe for the Great Australian Musical*, John Senczuk

PP43 *The Arts and the Common Good*, Katharine Brisbane

PP44 *Cultural Precincts: Art or commodity?* Justin Macdonnell

PP45 *Paying the Piper: There has to be another way*, Cathy Hunt

2016

PP46 *The Designer: Decorator or dramaturg?* Stephen Curtis

PP47 *Why We Need a Cultural Economy*, Justin O'Connor

PP48 *When the Goal Posts Move*, Ben Eltham

PP49 *The Lighting Designer: What is 'good' lighting*, Nigel Levings

2017

PP50 *Restless Giant: Changing cultural values in regional Australia*, Lindy Hume

PP51 *Missing in Action: The ABC and Australia's screen culture*, Kim Dalton

PP52 *Putting Words in their Mouths: The playwright and screenwriter at work*, Andrew Bovell

PP53 *The Jobbing Actor: Rules of engagement*, Lex Marinos

2018

PP54 *Young People and the Arts: An agenda for change*, Sue Giles

PP55 *Art, Politics, Money: Revisiting Australia's cultural policy*, David Throsby

PP56 *Falling Through the Gaps: Our artists' health and welfare*, Mark RW Williams

PP57 *Cultural Justice and the right to thrive*, Scott Rankin

2019

PP58 *The Changing Landscape of Australian Documentary*, Tom Zubrycki

PP59 *Ngarra-Burria: New music and the search for an Australian sound*, Christopher Sainsbury

PP60 *Capturing the Vanishing; A choreographer and film*, Sue Healey

PP61 *Criticism, Performance and the need for conversation*, Alison Croggon

2020

PP62 *Performing Arts Markets and their Conundrums*, Justin Macdonnell

2021

PP63 *On the Lessons of History*, Katharine Brisbane

COPYRIGHT INFORMATION

PLATFORM PAPERS
Quarterly essays from Currency House Inc.
Founding Editor: Dr John Golder
Editor: Katharine Brisbane
Currency House Inc. is a non-profit association and resource centre advocating the role of the performing arts in public life by research, debate and publication.

Postal address: PO Box 2270, Strawberry Hills, NSW 2012, Australia
Email: info@currencyhouse.org.au Tel: (02) 9319 4953
Website: www.currencyhouse.org.au Fax: (02) 9319 3649

ISBN 9781760626778
ISSN 1449-583X

Typeset in Garamond
Printed by Fineline Print + Copy Services, Revesby
Production by Currency Press Pty Ltd